CW01468783

PAGE 3

PAGE 4

Printed in Great Britain
by Amazon

16849109R00059